T0081140

Kids Can Help
ANIMALS

by Emily Raij

Consultant: Lisa Joyslin, Inclusive Volunteerism Program
Manager, Minnesota Association for Volunteer Administration,
St. Paul, Minnesota

CAPSTONE PRESS
a capstone imprint

Capstone Captivate is published by Capstone Press, an imprint of Capstone.
1710 Roe Crest Drive
North Mankato, Minnesota 56003
www.capstonepub.com

Library of Congress Cataloging-in-Publication Data is available on the Library of Congress website.
ISBN 978-1-4966-8375-5 (library binding)
ISBN 978-1-4966-8781-4 (paperback)
ISBN 978-1-4966-8426-4 (ebook pdf)

Summary: Make the world a better place for animals! This book is full of ideas and projects readers can put into action to help animals.

Image Credits
Getty Images: Orange County Register/Digital First Media/Leonard Ortiz, 15; Pixabay: Clker-Free-Vector-Images (paw), 14 (bottom), 19 (bottom), 20 (top), DavidZydd (stripe background), 1 and throughout; Shutterstock: a katz, 8, 23, 26, absolutimages, 13, BetterPhoto, 12, Cat-Bee, 27, Claire McAdams, 29 (top), Fototocam, 28 (top), Heder Zambrano, 14 (top), Inigo Sarralde Fotografia, 22, izzet ugutmen, 5, 6, Jennifer Bosvert, 20 (bottom), Lapina, 28 (bottom), Mega Pixel, 11, Monkey Business Images, cover, back cover, 7, 16, Motortion Films, 24, N. Antoine, 25, narikan, 18–19, Rich Carey, 17, SatawatK, 29 (bottom), Sean Xu, 29 (middle), serjiunea, 10, smilesbevie, 18, Stacy Ellen, 21, TippaPatt, 9, Vastram, 4

Editorial Credits
Editor: Erika L. Shores; Designer: Sara Radka; Media Researcher: Svetlana Zhurkin; Production Specialist: Tori Abraham

All internet sites appearing in back matter were available and accurate when this book was sent to press.

TABLE OF CONTENTS

Caring for Animals

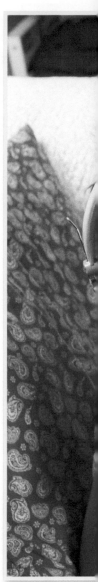

Do you have a favorite pet? Do you enjoy watching birds and other wildlife? Animals bring a lot of joy into people's lives. Having an animal can teach you about caring for living things. But not all animals get the care they need. Think about the animals in your community. Are there homeless dogs and cats? Can you think of animals or **habitats** nearby that are **endangered**? Maybe you have thought about helping to solve these problems. When you speak up for animals, you give them a voice. You also make your community a better place for every living thing, furry or not.

» Many towns and cities have homeless cats.

» Dog owners often have a special bond with their pets.

We know helping within our neighborhood or town makes a difference. In turn, it helps make a better world. We are being good global citizens. Solving problems facing animals in your community shows you care about living things beyond yourself.

What Can I Do?

What things do you care about? How do you like to help? Think about how you can use what you like doing to help animals. You might find that your knack for cooking or crafting comes in handy for several projects. Do you enjoy caring for plants or have a way with animals? Those skills will be useful too.

» If you love being around animals, you can work for causes that help make their lives better.

» If you like to bake, you can use that skill to help important causes.

You may feel like you have to fix a problem. But you don't need to be a hero. You can be a helper. That means you don't need to solve the whole problem. And you don't need to solve it right away. You just need to be part of the effort and work with others.

Charities are groups that raise money, collect goods, and provide **services** to those in need. These groups take care of immediate needs. These include food and shelter for animals. You can help an animal charity collect money and goods. Or you can **volunteer** directly to help animals in shelters.

» Animal charities hold events for people to meet animals waiting for new homes.

» Protecting bees is important for keeping the planet healthy.

Just like people, animals have the right to be healthy and safe in their homes. Fighting for animal rights shows you are **compassionate**. You are willing to help solve problems.

Caring for living things helps the global community. Healthy plants and animals are part of the life cycle. Bees **pollinate** flowers and plants. That keeps things growing. Trees suck water into the ground. That prevents floods.

Service Projects

HOMELESS AND SHELTER ANIMALS

Animal shelters or rescues are places where lost animals are kept safe. Sometimes owners give up their pet dogs and cats to a shelter when they can't care for them. Many shelters rely on **donations**. They have very little money to pay for much beyond animals' basic needs. You can make these places feel like home for scared and lonely animals.

» Some animals wait many months in a shelter before being adopted.

Dogs love treats! You can make homemade dog treats and donate them to a shelter. Some recipes use only a few ingredients. Others don't even involve baking, such as peanut butter balls you roll and refrigerate to harden.

Invite friends over for a baking party, and have fun while making a difference. Along with treats, collect old towels and blankets. Shelters need these for bathing and bedding. Be sure to call first to find out if the shelter accepts bedding and homemade treats. If they don't, you can sell the dog treats to neighbors and give the money to the shelter.

Recipes for Dog Treats

No-bake bites: Mix ⅔ cup no-sugar peanut butter, ⅓ cup carob powder, and 2 tablespoons shredded coconut. Roll the mixture into balls. Place them on a wax paper-lined tray, and refrigerate for two hours.

Three-ingredient canine cookies: Mix one ripe banana, ¼ cup canned pumpkin, and ½ cup coconut flour. Flatten the dough, and use cookie cutters to cut out fun shapes. Ask an adult to help you bake the cookies at 350 degrees Fahrenheit (177 degrees Celsius) for 20 minutes.

» By giving your time to shelter animals, you can help them learn to be good pets.

If you're looking for hands-on work, you may be able to help at a shelter. Sometimes you can work at pet adoption events. You can show people the pets waiting to be adopted and pass out forms. Some shelters let older kids volunteer with an adult. Your jobs may include washing and filling water and food bowls. You can also scoop litter boxes or clean up other messes.

If you have more animal experience, you might be able to walk dogs or brush and play with dogs and cats. Sometimes you can help train the dogs to sit or stay. These animals need kind people to keep them company.

Shelters can get overcrowded during disasters. Some animals get scared in bad weather. They may run away from their owners. Shelters need extra supplies for all these lost pets. Start a collection in your community to help shelters keep up during disasters. Be sure to put together emergency kits for all your pets. These keep your pets safe at home if power goes out and stores are closed.

Make a Disaster Kit for Pets

- food and water for at least five days for each pet, bowls, manual can opener for canned pet food
- medications and medical records stored in a waterproof container
- litter box, litter, and litter scoop
- bags for pet waste, paper towels, trash bags, bleach for cleaning up messes
- leashes, harnesses, and carriers
- collar and current ID tags (Pets should be wearing these.)
- blankets and towels
- a photo of you with your pets and descriptions of your pets
- printed information about feeding and behavior or medical issues

Another way to help shelters is to foster pets. If you have the space and your parents' OK, you can bring home a dog or cat. They can stay with you until they are adopted. This helps crowded shelters provide a safe space while animals wait for their forever home.

» Guinea pigs and other small pets sometimes need foster homes until they are adopted.

HELPING FACT

Speak up if you see animals being treated poorly. Ask an adult to call your local animal control agency if you see dogs chained up outside for hours without shade or water. Ask an adult to report dogs left in hot cars or too many animals in one home as well.

There are rescue groups and shelters for other animals too. Smaller pets such as rabbits, guinea pigs, snakes, turtles, and birds may need foster families. If you have cages and space for these animals, you can help foster them. You may discover a new favorite animal at the same time!

Emmy's Hope

When Emmy Perry of Southern California was 7 years old, she started a charity to help shelter animals. She wanted to encourage others to adopt homeless animals and donate items the shelters needed. Emmy's parents helped her set up a website, www.emmyshope.com, for donations. Her website also includes information on local shelters and where people can get help for their pets if they are affected by California's wildfires. For the past several years, Emmy has visited shelters to comfort animals and bring them food, blankets, and toys.

Animals Losing Their Habitats

Wild animals in your community may need help too. Habitat loss is a huge threat for wild animals. Swamps and forests are being cleared for houses and roads. Many habitats are also being turned into farmland. This destroys food sources and shelters for wild animals. As a result, some animals have become endangered or **extinct**. These include some species of frogs, birds, and fish.

» By learning about endangered animals, people can work to save them.

» Cutting down trees takes away homes for all kinds of wild animals.

You can help stop habitat loss where you live. Research which animals are endangered in your area. Then inform neighbors and friends. Make flyers with the names and photos of these animals. Include tips on protecting the animals. Suggest writing letters to the builders and companies destroying the habitats. Post the flyers on message boards in cafés, bookstores, and libraries.

Eagle Watching

People in 45 counties in Florida can take part in the Audubon EagleWatch through the Audubon Center for Birds of Prey. They visit the nests at least two times each month during nesting season. Then they turn in reports to the center. The reports inform the center on how the eagles are doing. Eagle watchers look for threats to nesting. Their reports can help protect the eagles. With more than 1,500 nesting pairs and 740 nests, these watchers stay busy!

Another way to help wildlife in your area is to plant **native** flowers and plants. Native plants give animals food and shelter. They also attract pollinators. These include bees, butterflies, and birds. That helps more plants and flowers grow. Visit a local garden center. Ask about the best native plants and flowers to grow. Find out when to plant them. Then find a spot and get gardening!

» Monarchs and other butterflies are important to pollination. By growing milkweed plants, people can bring more monarch butterflies to neighborhoods.

» Grow plants that are good for the animals and soil in an area.

Native plants not only attract wildlife, they also need less water and harmful **pesticides** than lawns. Fewer lawns mean less mowing. That means less air pollution from mowers. These plants and flowers also absorb more rain. They prevent flooding from water runoff that flows over grass or empty land.

HELPING FACT

Avoid using chemicals on your lawn and in your garden. These can make wildlife and pets sick if eaten. Make natural sprays from oils, soap, garlic, and pepper that keep plant-destroying weeds and insects away.

You can help birds right in your own backyard. Birds eat pests such as mosquitoes. They also help pollinate plants and flowers. You can make bird feeders to attract and feed backyard birds. Or set up birdbaths outside your home. This could also be a project you do at your school.

HELPING FACT

The World Wildlife Federation (WWF) lets you adopt endangered wildlife. You don't get to bring any animals home, but your donation helps the WWF protect wildlife habitats. Consider asking for donations toward adopting an animal instead of birthday presents.

» Setting up a birdbath is an easy way to help birds.

» Bird feeders are simple to make out of cardboard tubes.

There are some really simple bird feeder recipes. You can make most using things you already have at home. Save empty toilet paper and paper towel rolls. Spread peanut or sunflower butter on them. Then roll them in birdseed. Run a string through each tube. Hang your finished feeders from trees. Pinecones work well too. You can also use clean, empty milk cartons. Cut them in half, and fill them with birdseed. Do you have stale bagels and bread? Coat those with peanut butter and birdseed for feeders the birds can eat completely. Halved orange peels hold seeds too.

What If I Want to Do More?

   Activists work to change something unjust in the world. For example, they might work to pass a law to protect animals. They look at the big picture. They find out the deeper causes of problems. Activism can work to change things locally, nationally, or globally. Laws can be created or changed through city, state, or world leaders.

» Protests can help teach others about important problems.

» Some animal activists work to keep animals out of circuses, where they may be treated poorly.

You can be an animal rights activist. An animal activist might fight to protect endangered species by protesting their habitat destruction. For example, activists can set up a **rally**. They might protest the tearing down of a natural habitat to build offices or housing. The rally can help tell people about what animals are losing their homes and why.

Activism can be behind the scenes too. You do not have to be loud to make your voice heard. You can call, write to, or meet with lawmakers and companies. Ask them to change policies that hurt animals. Some of these harmful practices include testing products on animals. Puppy mills and animal abuse happen too. Laws can be made to stop people from running puppy mills. These places raise dogs in poor conditions and then sell them for high prices.

» Sending letters to lawmakers helps them learn about problems facing animals.

» A protest sign tells people to stop using animals in research.

Quiet activism includes writing a letter to the editor of a local newspaper. You can post on social media if a parent says it's OK. Pass out information at town meetings or community events. Attend a rally just to listen. Make and pass out protest signs. Activists make other people aware of an issue. They encourage others to take action.

Take Action

People and animals have a connection. But animals cannot speak for themselves. They need our help. We can protect their rights to a safe and healthy life.

Saving Paws
Rescue, Inc

bestfriends.org

» Bringing attention to animal charities is one way to help animals.

» A volunteer feeds a homeless kitten.

Whether you want to help animals at a shelter or protect wildlife habitats, there are many projects available. Find one that makes good use of your time and talent. Think of what you care about. Think of what you like to do. You can work on your own or with a group. No kid or action is too small when it comes to improving the lives of animals.

Other Ways to Help

» Organize a collection drive to get items on a local shelter's list of needs.

» Be a Rescue Reader. Rescue Readers is a program at many animal adoption centers. Kids in this program can read to dogs or cats. This calms the animals while helping kids feel good about reading out loud.

» Hold an information night letting neighbors know why it's important to spay and neuter pets. Spaying and neutering animals keeps them from having babies. That can keep more pets from becoming homeless.

» Have a charity dog wash. People can bring their dogs to get bathed for a donation to a local shelter. Ask for donations of soap, towels, and buckets for the wash. Give those to the shelter after the event.

» Make a video explaining why it's important to microchip your cat or dog and put ID tags on their collars. Then ask to show the video on your school website or submit it to your local news stations.

» Plan a dog park cleanup day to keep parks clean and safe for everyone to enjoy.

» Set up a butterfly garden in your backyard. These gardens have plants that attract and feed butterflies. In turn, the butterflies pollinate the plants.

» Only have a few minutes? Visit www.freekibble.com to donate free pet food to shelters for every question you answer.

Glossary

activist (AC-tiv-ist)—a person who works for social or political change

charity (CHAYR-uh-tee)—a group that raises money or collects goods to help people or animals in need

compassionate (kuhm-PASH-uh-nyt)—being concerned for someone in trouble that leads to the desire to help

donation (doh-NAY-shun)—money or goods given as a present

endangered (in-DAYN-juhrd)—at risk of dying out

extinct (ik-STINGKT)—no longer living; an extinct animal is one that has died out, with no more of its kind

habitat (HAB-uh-tat)—the natural place and conditions in which a plant or animal lives

native (NAY-tuhv)—growing or living naturally in a particular place

pesticide (PEST-uh-side)—a poisonous chemical used to kill insects, rats, and fungi that can damage plants

pollinate (pol-uh-NAYT)—to move pollen from flower to flower; pollination helps flowers make seeds

rally (RAL-ee)—an organized event where people join together to help a person or thing

service (SUR-viss)—a helpful or useful activity or action

volunteer (vol-uhn-TIHR)—to offer to do something without pay

Read More

Gianferrari, Maria. *Operation Rescue Dog.* New York: Little Bee Books, 2018.

Jackson, Tom. *Saving Animal Species.* North Mankato, MN: Capstone, 2018.

Papp, Lisa. *Madeline Finn and the Shelter Dog.* Atlanta: Peachtree Publishing Company, 2019.

Internet Sites

Endangered Species
www.fws.gov/endangered/

Mission Animal Rescue
kids.nationalgeographic.com/explore/nature/mission-animal-rescue/

Save Animals
www.petakids.com/save-animals/

Index